Mr. Wulff's Eagle-Powered Balloon
and other aviation ideas from the U.S. Patent Office

by

Curt Dalton

To the Wingers,

Curt Dalton

Hawthorn Hill

7/17/03

Also by Curt Dalton

Breweries of Dayton: A Toast to Brewers from the Gem City 1810 to 1961
Greater Dayton Drive-In Movie Theaters
Home Sweet Home Front: Dayton During World War II
How Ohio Helped Invent the World: From the Airplane to the Yo-yo
The Terrible Resurrection
Through Flood, Through Fire: Personal Stories from Survivors of the Dayton
        Flood of 1913
When Dayton Went to the Movies

ISBN   0-9715702-7-2

Curt Dalton
2058 Ottello Avenue
Dayton, OH 45414
email: cdalton@woh.rr.com

Introduction

Before the Wright Brothers, there were far more failures than fliers when it came to airplane designs submitted to the U.S. Patent Office.

Mr. Wulff was a tinkerer who, in 1887, sent off his immortal design for a guidance apparatus for aerial ships. His idea was to replace the mechanical motor with a living one, that of a bird. And not just any bird, but those he considered from the "flying class", his examples being eagles, vultures and condors. The idea seemed reasonable to the official government examiners, who granted Mr. Wulff patent number 363,037.

As bird-brain as Wulff's idea sounds, it doesn't compare to Watson F. Quinby's design of a man with wings and tail feathers attached to his body who was supposed to use them to "swim" through the air.

Edwin Pyncheon's "flying ship" also had an unusual means of propulsion. After some degree of ascent and forward motion had been obtained, a pair of small cartridges containing gun powder would be detonated behind the vessel, the force of the explosion pushing it forward. This would be followed by other explosions of ever increasing force until the ship reached cruising speed. This, in itself, would have been dangerous. Seeing that a balloon full of flammable hydrogen gas was what helped keep the aircraft afloat takes the idea a step further to plain zany.

Step inside and take a look at aerial patents submitted to the United States Patent Office that never got off the ground - and some that did!

Contents

M. NELSON.
AERIAL CAR.

No. 32,378.

Patented May 21, 1861.

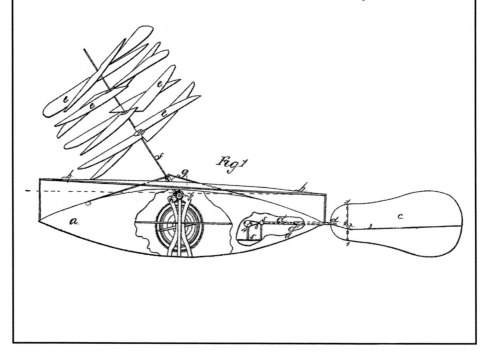

Fig 1

Mortimer Nelson
U. S. Patent 32,378
New York, NY
May 21, 1861

Nelson's "aerial car" is thought to be the earliest record of an American attempt to build a helicopter. The combination helicopter-balloon airship consisted of a body with tapering ends, a pear-shaped rudder at the stern, a parachute canopy over the top of the fuselage and two vertical shafts rising out of the body. Fans were attached to the rotors, both being arranged so that "when the shafts stand vertically ... the revolution of them will tend to raise the balloon or car and that when they are inclined forward their action on the air will give propulsion to the car. " Nelson foresaw the invention of the convertiplane by almost a century.

The rudder was fashioned in such a way that it could control the craft's upward, downward, and sidewise flying directions. The parachute above the car sat at an angle and served the same purpose as a wing to give the craft lift. According to Nelson, the parachute "gives sustaining power to the car in moving through the air and forms a buoyant sail."

The car was designed to be attached to a balloon filled with gas in order to help the device get into the air. Once airborne, the fans and rudder gave the pilot complete control of the ship's direction.

Unfortunately, Nelson was unable to give his invention a whirl, as it was never built.

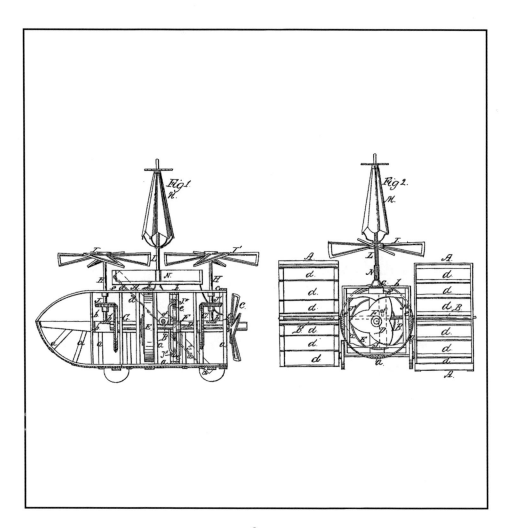

Watson F. Quinby

U. S. Patent 33,797
Stanton, DE
November 26, 1861

Dr. Quinby left his practice in Alabama, and headed to California during the gold rush of 1849. It was this love of adventure that led him to design several machines with the idea of solving the problem of aerial navigation.

Quinby's helicopter did away with the use of a balloon. His concept consisted of a "boat-like" car made of wood covered with oiled silk. A pair of oblong oscillating wings, one on each side of the car, were fitted with flaps that opened when the vehicle rose and closed as it descended. A screw-propeller, located in the back, could propel the craft in a horizontal direction. The main shaft controlled the movement of the wings, as well as the upright shafts of the two spiral-bladed wheels above the car that assisted in controlling the ascent, descent and elevation of the ship. As the shaft rotated, the wings would move up and down. On the downward swing, the flaps on the wings would close; causing a resistance that would help lift the machine. As the wings rose upward, the flaps would open, lessening the wind resistance.

Once airborne the pilot would turn on the screw-propeller for propulsion. The wings could then be locked in a forward inclination, causing the apparatus to rise even farther. To descend the wings would be locked in a horizontal position. The spiral-bladed wheels would help control the descent at this point, as did the umbrella-like structure standing between the two wheels, which could be spread open to act like a parachute.

Quinby's flying machine never made it past the design stage.

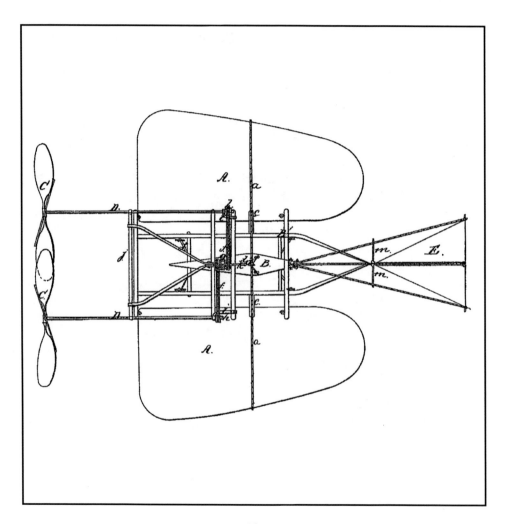

Luther C. Crowell
U. S. Patent 35,437
West Dennis, MA
June 3, 1862

Luther C. Crowell's patent called for propellers fastened to shafts that could be swung from a vertical position to a horizontal one. When ascending, the propellers would be above the ship's body. For forward movement the propellers were lowered to a horizontal position. The propellers would be driven by a steam engine, fitted in the compartment next to the pilot.

The wings were adjustable as well. For up and down flight the wings would be locked in a vertical position. After reaching the desired altitude, the pilot would lock them horizontally for flying in a forward direction. The wings were covered with a cloth impervious to air or gas, with a hollow space of two or three feet between the top and bottom of the coverings. When ready for flight, this hollow area was to be filled with hydrogen gas to help lighten the burden the wings and rotors would have to carry. The machine could be steered in any direction by a pyramid-shaped rudder fixed to the stern of the fuselage. A set of cords and pulleys allowed the pilot complete control of the craft.

The beginning of the Civil War undoubtedly influenced Crowell to design his airship. In his patent he states that "when it is desirable to employ this aerial machine as an engine of war, it could be elevated, loaded with shell, and when it arrived over the desired spot the shell could be discharged." This effectively describes the use airplanes would be given during World War I a half-century later.

Crowell's invention was never built, maybe because any pilot cooped up that close to a steam engine would have been scalded by the heat.

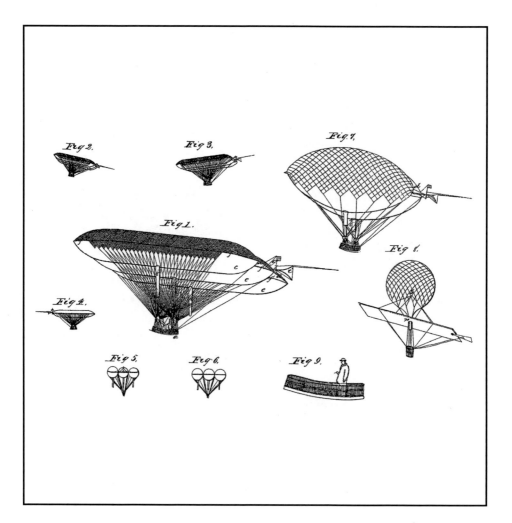

Solomon Andrews
U. S. Patent 43,449
Perth Amboy, NJ
July 5, 1864

Forty years before the Wright Brothers flew Solomon Andrews invented the first self-propelled balloon that could be steered. Named the *Aereon*, the airship consisted of three parallel cigar-shaped balloons, each cylinder being 80 feet long and 13 feet in diameter. The balloons were tied together with ropes and had a wicker basket suspended below, as well as a rudder for steering.

The *Aereon* made its maiden voyage over Perth Amboy on June 1, 1863. It performed so well in following experiments that Andrews wrote President Abraham Lincoln, his thoughts being that the ship could be used to help defeat the Confederates during the Civil War. Lincoln was intrigued enough to meet with Andrews, who shortly thereafter demonstrated the *Aereon* before a military committee. They were less than impressed it seems, as it took them a year to tell Andrews that they were not interested in pursuing the idea.

Andrews decided to start the Aerial Navigation Company, with the thought of building more airships and using them to transport people and items back and forth from New York to Philadelphia. In order to advertise his service, he flew over New York City on May 25, 1865. This proved to be so popular that he again flew his ship over the city on June 5, landing at Oyster Bay, Long Island.

Unfortunately, in post war panic, hundreds of banks failed and the Aerial Navigation Company had to close its doors.

Andrews other inventions include a sewing machine, a gas lamp and a padlock. He also served three terms as Mayor of Perth Amboy.

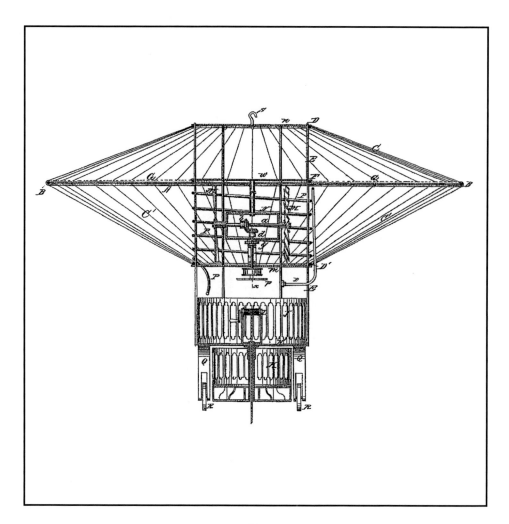

John Wooton
U. S. Patent 54,992
Boonton, NJ
May 22, 1866

Wooton's aircraft featured a large ring-shaped parachute beneath which hung two circular compartments. Two propellers, situated under the parachute, were powered by a steam engine located in the upper compartment. Wooton did not believe that his propellers would be powerful enough to actually lift the machine into the sky. Instead, the ship was to be hauled up an inclined railway, then released. The force of gravity would allow the apparatus to slide down the incline and up the next as well, where it would then soar into the air. He believed that this would be enough of a lift for the propellers to take over and keep the vessel in the air.

Once the craft was in the air, the bottom compartment was rigged so it could be raised or lowered. This enabled passengers to board while the rest of the ship remained airborne.

Stopping the machine seemed to be even more dangerous that starting it. Designed to descend vertically, Wooton proposed to erect a set of high posts between which ropes were stretched. The pilot was supposed to direct the ship so that the ropes would come in contact with a hook on top of the aircraft, halting its flight.

Wooton's UFO-like design was never built here on Earth...

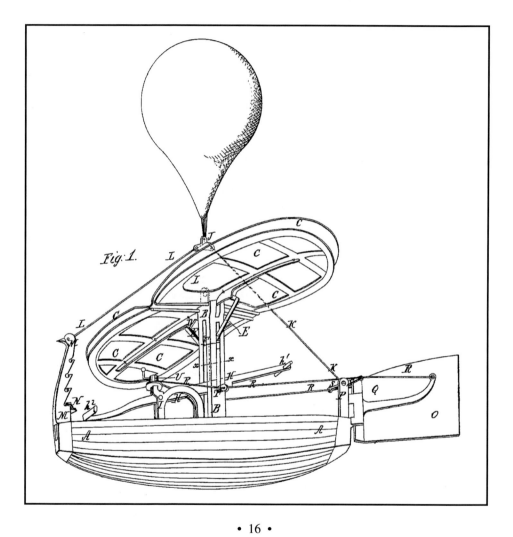

Fig. 1.

J. A. Elston
U. S. Patent 67,739
Station, MO
August 18, 1867

Although Elston added wings to his balloon, he still shaped the machine as if it was for traveling through water instead of air.

"I prefer to make (the car) boat-shaped," states the inventor in his patent, "so as to encounter less resistance in moving through the air, and so as to be more under control of the rudder."

A pair of concave wings could be made to move up and down, "similar to that of a bird's wings in flying", by two men operating a lever shaped like a teeter-totter. Above the wings stood a balloon, designed to merely take the brunt of the weight of the airship, allowing the wings to be able to cause the craft to rise. The car below was attached by a series of ropes, pulleys and eye-blocks so that the forward end of the car could be raised or lowered as desired.

The wings would be used until the desired height was reached. When the desired direction was made, the pilot would begin to descend by lowering the front end of the car. Gravity and the rudder would take care of forward speed and control of direction, something that would not be possible if the machine simply floated in the wind. If the ship's destination had not been reached by the time it neared the ground, the entire process of beating the wings, pointing the ship and descending was to be repeated. To land, the forward end of the car would be raised above the level of the rear end. The force of the wings would then be downward and forward, breaking the momentum of the vessel. Shaped like a Viking's dream-boat, Elston's device never left shore.

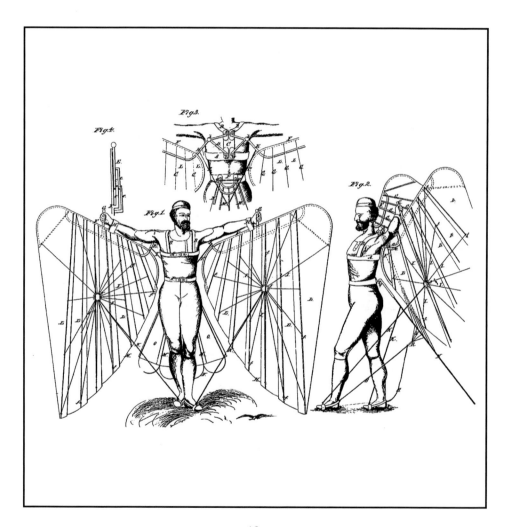

Watson F. Quinby

U. S. Patent 68,789
Wilmington, DE
September 10, 1867

After receiving a patent for a helicopter-type craft in 1861 (see page 8), Quinby began experimenting with the idea of self-propelled flight.

His first attempt consisted of two side wings and one dorsal wing, constructed in a way that they could be operated by the combined actions of the pilots' arms and legs. The frames of the wings were made of wood or metal tubing. Rods of cane were secured to the frames. A strip of oiled silk was attached to each rod, each strip being large enough to slightly overlap the rod next to it. The rods were arranged to allow air to pass through freely during the upward stroke of the wings and close during the downstroke.

"In using this invention, a motion is given the arms and legs almost precisely like that in swimming, and the effect is nearly the same," stated Quinby in his patent, "the difference in density between water and air being compensated by the greater extent presented by the wings in the one case over the hands and feet in the other."

Quinby later obtained two other patents on the same principle, making adjustments in braces, belts and wings in his attempt to have man fly using only his own strength. Gravity proved too strong and man too weak for the idea to take full flight.

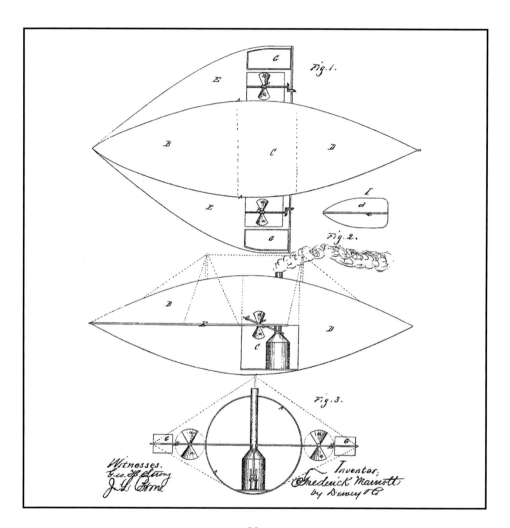

Fig. 1.

Fig. 2.

Fig. 3.

Witnesses.
Geo. H. Strong
J. S. Stone

Inventor,
Frederick Marriott
by Dewey & Co.

Frederick Marriott

U. S. Patent 97,100
San Francisco, CA
November 23, 1869

Although he has been nearly forgotten by almost everyone but the most dedicated of aviation historians, Marriott's contribution to flight was an important one. While living in England he helped publicize William S. Henson's work on his airship, the Henson Aerial Stream Carriage.

Marriott was enticed to come to America by the possibility of striking it rich during the Gold Rush in California. This didn't happen, but he did manage to establish his own newspaper a few years later. He also managed to acquire enough funds to build a model of his airship, which he called *Avitor Hermes, Jr.* The aircraft consisted of a balloon powered by a steam engine, which was used to turn two screw propellers. The *Avitor, Jr.* was meant to be a smaller test version of the full-size passenger ship he hoped to build later.

On July 2, 1869, at Shellmound Park across the bay from San Francisco, a crowd watched as the balloon was given a series of tethered tests. The unmanned machine became airborne and was able to complete two half-mile circles at about six miles an hour. This feat is generally considered the first powered flight of a lighter-than-air craft in the United States. The model burned sometime thereafter and was never rebuilt.

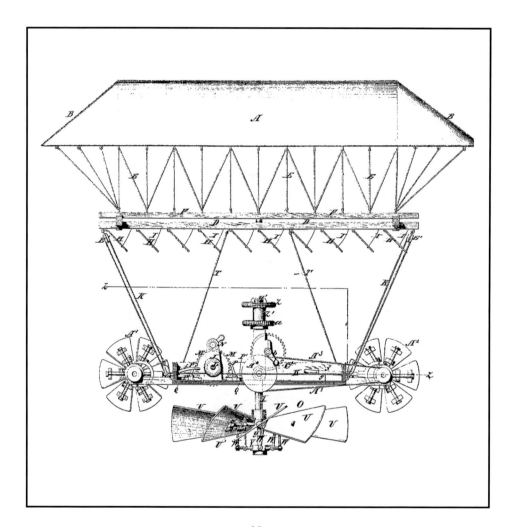

Edward Oakes
U. S. Patent 106,862
Richmond, IN
August 30, 1870

Edward Oakes' invention consisted of a car attached to one or more semi-cylindrical balloons with pointed ends and flat bottoms. The balloon was to be made of the usual material of varnished silk or rubber cloth, except for the bottom part, which was to be covered by a plate of lightweight metal.

The balloon was attached to a sail. The sail consisted of a rectangular frame of wood and metal, to the under side of which was connected a series of flaps made of vulcanized India rubber. The flaps were hinged at their forward edges to the frame, the other ends having cords that could be used to hold the flaps at a forty-five degree angle during the ship's lift-off.

Underneath the aerial car was a set of blades attached to a shaft, which Oakes called a "lifting wheel". The balloon was not to be large enough to lift the weight of the machine by itself, but just enough to enable the car to take off vertically after the lifting-wheel was engaged. This allowed the ship to descend under its own weight when the lifting-wheel was disengaged.

In order to control the direction of the aircraft, the pilot was advised to apply power to the lifting-wheel until he reached an altitude of sufficient height, then begin to descend rapidly in the direction he wanted to travel. When sufficient momentum was achieved in the direction the pilot wanted to travel, the aerial machine was to be leveled off. Guiding wheels at the front and back of the vessel helped keep it on course. When the forward movement of the ship was expended, the pilot merely had to repeat the above procedure.

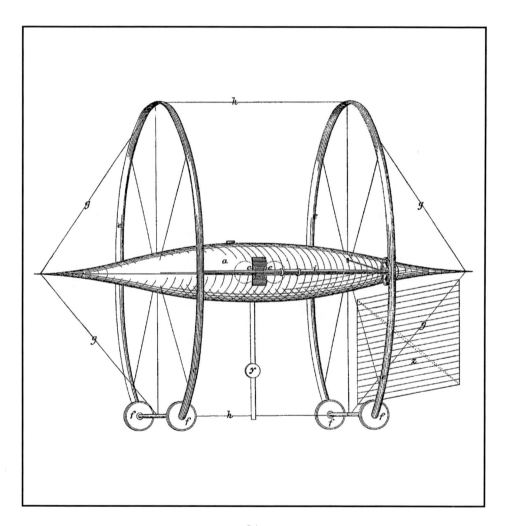

Thomas Moy & Richard E. Shill
U. S. Patent 133,381
London and Mile End, England
November 26, 1872

Thomas Moy and Richard Shill's invention consisted of two six-bladed propellers, each of six-foot diameter, placed side-by-side between the two main planes of the machine that spanned fifteen feet. A third steering plane, of smaller size, was placed in the rear to serve as a horizontal rudder. All of this was supported on a triangle wheeled undercarriage. The craft was powered by an eighty-pound steam engine that had been built specifically for it by Moy and Shill.

In June 1875, Moy and Shill tested their giant ship in the great Crystal Palace in London, England. The "Moy Aerial Steamer", as it was called, was tethered to a post in the center of a specially built circular track. The ground surface was gravel, which proved to be too rough, shaking the aeroplane. Then a boardwalk was laid over the path, which improved matters. The next problem came from the steam engine, which used six Russian lamps burning methylated spirits for power. When running in the open air, the fumes from the three forward lamps extinguished the three lamps behind them, effectively cutting the power of the engine by half. Although it reached a speed of twelve miles an hour, this was not fast enough to actually achieve flight (there are conflicting reports that claim the aircraft managed to lift six-inches off the ground).

Moy proposed to build an even larger apparatus, with a 100 horsepower engine capable of producing the speed needed. Moy's dream came to an end when he found that no one was interested in funding future experiments.

Otto Francis
U. S. Patent 147,252
Grand Rapids, MI
February 10, 1874

Francis' aircraft was shaped like a ship, which he claimed was to "enable the air to be navigated with the same facility as is now afforded by vessels plying upon the water."

The hull was constructed to be shaped in the same way as would be required to sail the seven seas. Within the hull were placed a number of pear-shaped balloons that were to contain the gas needed to raise and sustain the load of the airship. At the lower side of the interior of the hull were arranged a number of water tanks for supplying ballast, each tank having a valve that could be controlled to discharge the water when necessary.

The vessel was propelled, in part, by a system of sails that were arranged and operated in the usual manner of a ship at sea. Fan wheels, which protruded from the sides of the machine, revolved vertically and helped to guide the movement of the aircraft. A rudder was hinged or pivoted to the stern of the hull, which also provided a means to steer the craft left and right.

Additional means for assisting in the operation of the apparatus was furnished by a set of canvas wings, which extended outward and downward from the sides of the hull. A portion of each wing could be moved downward until its lower edge was in line with the keel. This was used to prevent the ship from tilting to either side when it was at rest on the ground.

Like so many inventions of this type, what looked good on paper was also a waste of the same. Francis' invention was never built.

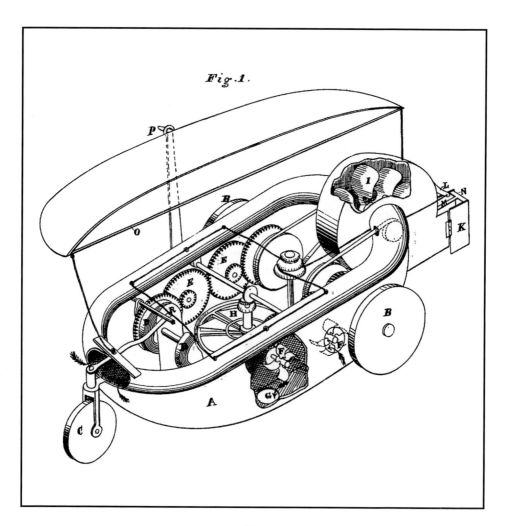

Fig. 1.

John B. Ward
U. S. Patent 185,465
San Francisco, CA
December 19, 1876

The style of Ward's machine was not specified in his patent, his only comment that it be "made of any suitable shape and material, so that it will be light and strong, such as thin metal properly braced, bamboo or wood." He also recommended the use of wheels, which would " support it when it starts upon the surface, until it has acquired a speed sufficient to allow... it to leave the surface and move through the air." The device also had a steering wheel so it could be guided like a car while on the surface.

Keeping his options open, Ward gave several suggestions on how the ship could be powered. The driving force being shown in the drawing consisted of large springs. An arched "wing" was to be attached to the top of the aircraft. A wheel, with vanes that could be opened and closed at will, was to be fitted to rotate in the center, acting as a gyroscope and giving assistance in lifting the vehicle during flight.

Wooton's concept anticipated modern jet lift and jet propulsion airplanes. When set in motion, a blower fan located at the rear of the vehicle would drive the craft forward. Once a certain speed was reached, a series of fan-blowers constructed in cases at the sides of the airship would be turned on, discharging air in a vertical direction through openings at the bottom of the machine. The front of the wing would be inclined upward. Once in flight, direction could be controlled by hinged gates at the end of the rear blower, which moved from side to side.

Ward's modern design was too far ahead of its time, and never built.

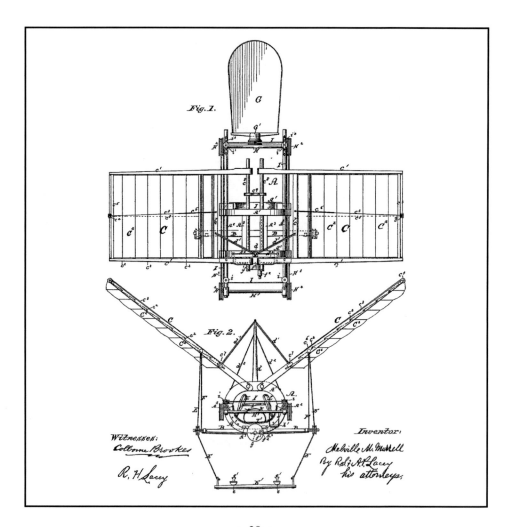

Fig.1.

Fig.2.

Witnesses:
Colborne Brookes

R. H. Lacey

Inventor:
Melville M. Murrell
By Rob. A. Lacey
his attorneys.

Melville M. Murrell

U. S. Patent 194,104
Panther Springs, TN
August 14, 1877

According to family legend, Murrell's first attempt to fly involved flapping cabbage leaves while jumping from a stone wall at his Panther Springs home in Tennessee. Undaunted by his lack of success, the young boy carved models of flying machines and never gave up the hope that one day he would fly.

By 1876 Murrell had succeeded in building an ornithopter, a fancy term for an aircraft that flies by flapping its wings like a bird. The wings were divided into slats that opened for the least air resistance on the way up and closed on the way down for maximum lift.

Charlie Cowan, a hired hand on the Murrell farm, was the first to fly the machine. The device was controlled by a series of cords and pulleys; the flapping was accomplished by the pilot repeatedly flexing his legs. Although it was in the air for only a few seconds before it crashed, Murrell's invention did get off the ground.

Excited, Murrell wrote off a letter to a friend in Dakota, stating "I can now say 'Eureka, Eureka,' for it works like a charm." He was granted a patent for his airship the following year.

Murrell would later invent another airplane, this one powered by a motorcycle engine. He never succeeded in getting it off the ground.

In 1928, for reasons unknown, Murrell destroyed his inventions by setting them on fire. A few parts escaped destruction, including the wings of the first plane, which are on display at the Rose Center, in Morristown, TN.

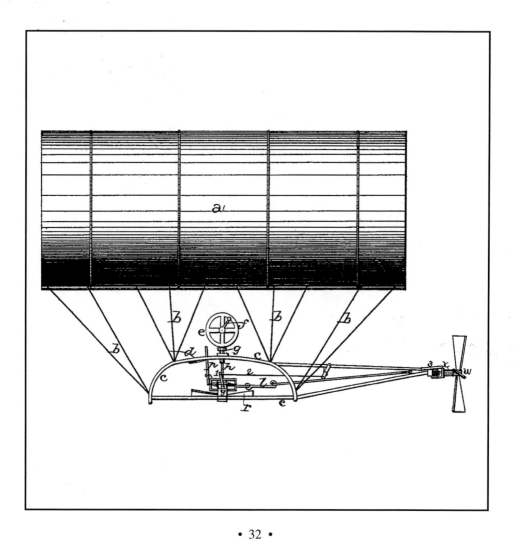

Charles F. Ritchel
U. S. Patent 201,200
Corry, PA
March 12, 1878

Ritchel's airship consisted of a balloon tied to a framework of "light, strong rods" and braces. Supported on two of the crossbars of the frame was a seat on which the pilot sat. At the front of the frame was a propeller wheel that could be pivoted in any direction. Another "lifting" propeller wheel (designated by the letter r in the drawing) was connected to the bottom of the framework.

In the middle of the vehicle was the main driving-wheel which, by means of gears, shafts and a clutch, were connected to both the front and bottom propeller wheels. This would be cranked by the pilot, allowing him control of the ascent or descent of the aircraft, as well as the direction he wanted to travel.

The "Ritchel Flying-Machine" was demonstrated to the public several times in May and June of 1878. The final version had a gas-bag made of rubberized material and a framework constructed of brass tubing. The flights were a success. In at least in two instances the pilot was able to remain in the air for over an hour. The machine was taken to several states, including Connecticut, Massachusetts and Pennsylvania, and made the first outdoor, public powered flight in the United States, as well as the first outdoor, public powered circular flight in the United States. Due to this success, Ritchel was able to build and sell five of his "Flying Machines."

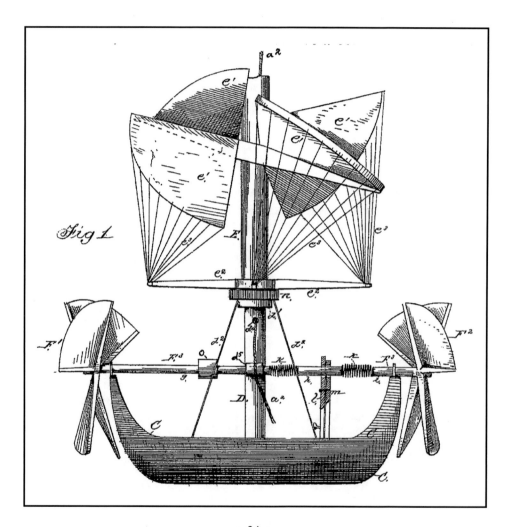

Fig 1

Henry Badgley
U. S. Patent 214,546
Fairfax Court-House, VA
October 1, 1878

Badgley's aerial machine had a propeller on the front end that was used to move it forward and backward. The rear propeller could be swiveled for the purpose of steering. From the center of the aircraft stood a mast, carrying at its upper end a cylindrical balloon (not shown in the drawing). A horizontal "lifting" propeller below helped supplement the balloon in raising the airship. The car below held the steam engine that powered the three propellers, as well as the pilot and passengers.

Badgley made a point in his patent that the balloon used by the machine could be of any desired shape, but its lifting capacity was to only be large enough to *almost* lift the car, the steam engine and whatever persons were aboard. "By thus giving the balloon such a lifting power all the more force may be applied to driving the machine back and forth and from side to side."

Although it never succeeded in taking off, Badgley's design caused enough of a stir in the imagination that a drawing of it appeared in a magazine in 1879, along with other aerial ships that were thought to depict the future of flight.

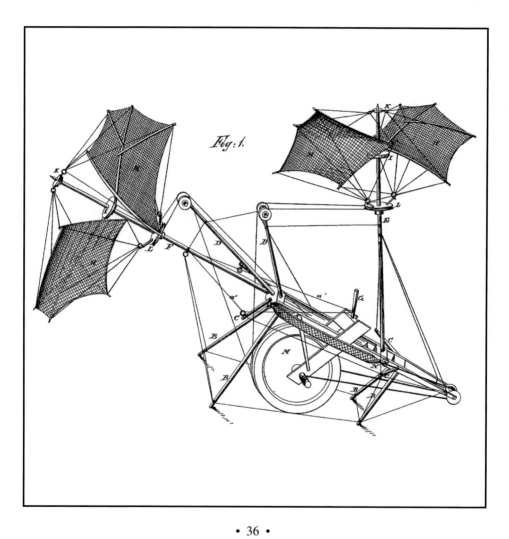

Fig: 1.

Watson F. Quinby

U. S. Patent 218,573
Wilmington, DE
August 12, 1879

Eighteen years after his first try at a helicopter-type aircraft, Quinby again attempted to take to the air. His rotorcraft had four rigid legs for the landing gear, an inclined body, and a long nose boom to which were fastened two small sails for a propeller. The lifting propeller or rotor was also made of a pair of small sails, which whirled around a vertical shaft, above the body of the machine.

The sails consisted of fabric attached to a light framework of rods. When power was applied to the main pulley, a combination of cords, belts and ropes transferred the movement to the wings, making them revolve. The lifting propeller would then make the vehicle rise, while the sails on the front would draw the ship forward.

There appeared to be only one problem with Quinby's design, but it was a major one. Nowhere in the patent does he mention what was to be used to power his invention. The drawing does not seem to leave enough room for even a man to sit and propel the machine with his legs, let alone the possibility of attaching a steam engine to turn the main pulley. Unfortunately, Quinby's craft seems like a waste of a couple of good umbrellas.

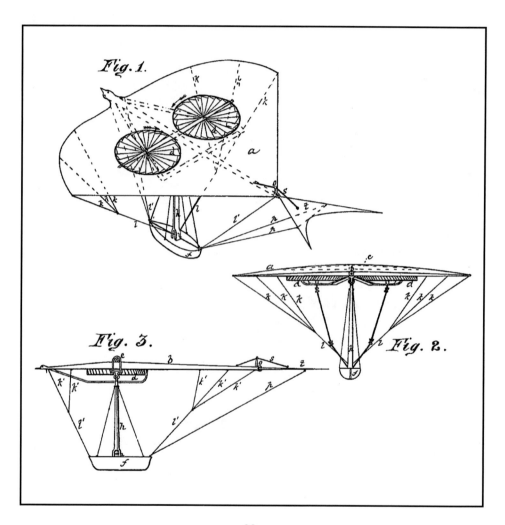

Fig.1.

Fig.3.

Fig.2.

John J. Greenough
U. S. Patent 220,473
Syracuse, NY
October 14, 1879

In 1842, while living in Washington, DC Greenough was granted the first patent in America for a sewing machine. His idea combined a stitch forming mechanism with a device for presenting work to a double pointed needle with an eye in the middle. But, even though a model was made and exhibited, no one was interested enough to manufacture Greenough's invention.

Thirty-seven years later Greenough designed what he called an "Aerobat". One glance at his patent drawing shows that his bat-shaped aircraft was aptly named. The wing's framework was to be made of any light material, such as bamboo. It was to be covered with a strong, light tissue that was impervious to air, and both waterproof and fireproof for safety.

The airship's two lifting rotors whirled around in two large circular openings cut into the wings. These "wind-wheels" revolved in opposite directions, driven by a steam engine in the body below. Greenough recommended that the blades be constructed in such a way that they closed up to prevent any upward current of wind through them when the pressure upward was greater than the downward current.

The "tail", or rudder, was shaped like a triangle and joined with a universal joint to the rear of the backbone of the ship. This design enabled the pilot to move in any direction he might require. A boat-shaped fuselage was suspended beneath the wing.

Unfortunately, the combine weight of an iron steam engine, the wood needed to stoke it, a pilot and the ship itself made the idea a little"batty".

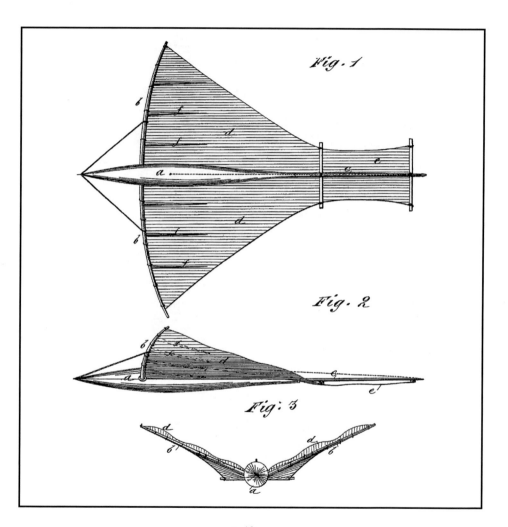

Fig. 1

Fig. 2

Fig. 3

Frederick W. Brearey

U. S. Patent 234,947
Blackheath, County of Kent, England
November 30, 1880

In 1880, Brearey patented the idea for an aircraft that had flexible fabric attached to a central spine, as well as vibrating wing arms at the front, which beat up and down like the wings of a bird. This would throw the fabric into a state of wavelike motions, which caused the machine to rise up into the air. The engine used to power the wings was to be placed in the body attached to the central spine. The apparatus was to either be mounted on wheels, or made watertight in order to float in water when it landed.

Brearey wrote that he took the idea for his design from watching the movements of a "skate" fish in an aquarium, which in swimming undulated its entire body. He found that when applied to propulsion in air, the loose fabric acted like a parachute, allowing the vehicle to come down safely if the power source failed. The pilot controlled the craft's descent by moving forward or backward in the car, or by pulling a cord attached to the tail.

The inventor's idea, like most of those based on trying to imitate nature in flight, failed.

Brearey was one of the most successful inventors of flying models, if not actual full-sized machines. He would give experimental lectures, using large models that could flap their wings to illustrate his point, one model being 6 feet wide by 10 feet long. Due more to these accomplishments, he was made Honorary Secretary of the Royal Aeronautical Society of Great Britain from 1865 to around 1895.

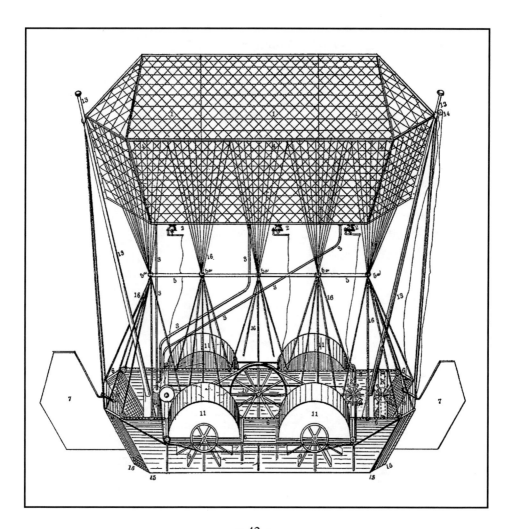

Charles A. Sullivan
U. S. Patent 235,040
Starkville, MS
November 30, 1880

Sullivan's balloon looked for all the world like the paddle-wheeled boats he must have watched cruise up and down the Mississippi River.

The lifting power was hydrogen gas, which was to be contained in one or more balloons that sat above the riding car. Each balloon was divided into compartments, so that if gas escaped from one section, it would not impair the safety of the airship.

The balloons were attached to the car below with a network of strong twine, which was fastened on either side to stay ropes and rods, where they were again fastened to another large stay rope and rod, which ran parallel with the bottom of the balloon. The ropes all concentrating at points in line with each other were supposed to act like a hinge, the idea being that the car would remain stable even if the balloons above were disturbed by a sudden gust of wind.

The car was equipped with four large fan wheels, two on each side. The axle of the wheels extended all the way across the car, one axle serving two wheels. A large wheel in the center of the vessel controlled the forward and backward movement of the paddle-wheel shaped fans which, in turn, propelled the aerostat in that direction.

No one wanted to gamble on Sullivan's steam-boat design, so it was never built.

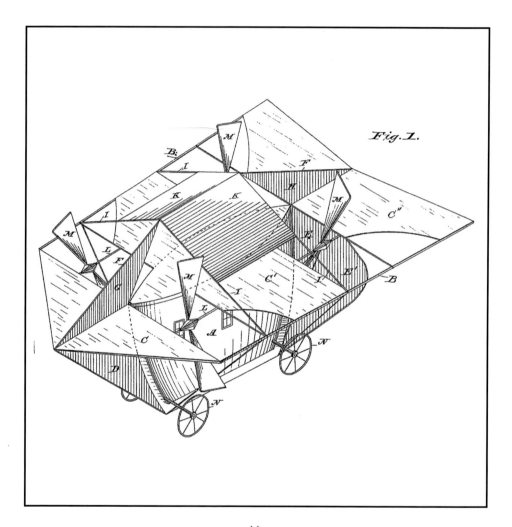

Fig. 1.

William G. Krueger
U. S. Patent 252,955
St. Louis, MO
January 31, 1882

Although Krueger stated in his patent that his object was to construct an airship or flying machine that could carry passengers or freight, etc., it actually involved building a frame around already existing vessels which would enable them to fly.

First you would begin with any aircraft made of a light and strong material. Krueger recommended that the ship be "made narrow, deep and long" in order to cut down air resistance. The size could be varied according to the number of passengers or the amount to be transported. To this "vessel" would be attached Krueger's invention, which consisted of a very strong frame with horizontal and vertical planes attached to it. The horizontal planes supported the vehicle while in the air. The vertical planes, hinged to the stern and bow of the airship, controlled the direction of travel. On each side of the craft, in suitable bearings in the frame, were propellers. The propellers were made broader at their outer ends than at their inner ends, and were spiral shaped "so as to act against the air when revolving, similarly to an ordinary propeller revolving in the water." These were to be powered by a mechanism inside the aircraft, although no mention is made as to what this was.

Arranged over the central part of the ship were arched planes that, in case of an accident, would act as a parachute and stop its descent . These could also be contracted or extended, helping guide the aircraft up and down. The frame also provided the vessel with wheels that were used during take-off, a feature that turned out to be unnecessary, as it never left the ground.

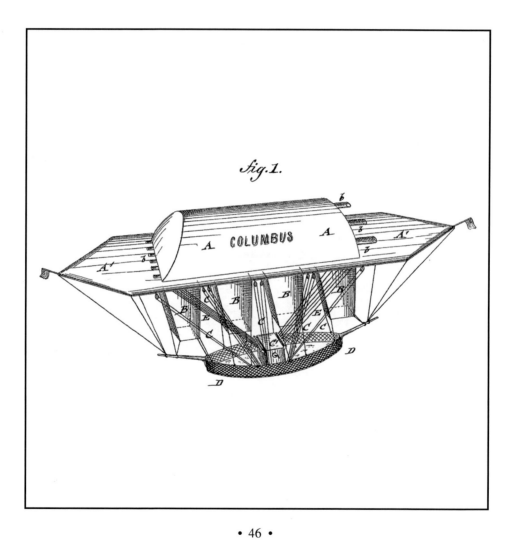

Fig.1.

COLUMBUS

Charles P. Fest

U. S. Patent 263,397
Philadelphia, PA
August 29, 1882

Fest's invention used the method of heated air to lift his airship. Although the source of the fuel that provided the heat was not specified, the "burning-fluid" was put in a receptacle in the car. The receptacle contained a grooved cylinder that revolved, around which wick-cords were passed. As the endless wick-cords passed through the receptacle they became saturated with fuel. These wick-cords were then guided in fixed inclined wick-tubes, which extended from the car below to each end of the balloon above. There, the wick was not enclosed in a wick-tube, so it could be ignited to heat the air in the balloon.

The elongated body of the aircraft was tapered at the front and rear ends, so that it offered as little resistance as possible to the air it was traveling in. The bottom of the body was to be made flat and provided with several openings, all of which were capable of being closed when needed. When the ship reached the desired height, air from outside could be slowly let in, which would stop the upward process of the balloon. The vehicle would then float in the air because of the resistance of the air exerted on the extended flat bottom of the balloon. Tubes (marked *B* in the drawing) could be used to release heated air, the force of which could be employed for steering the ship.

Fest's invention never left the drawing stage, so no one knows if the wick-tubes would have completely extinguished the fire in the wick before it reached the container of fuel, or if the airship would have gone down in flames.

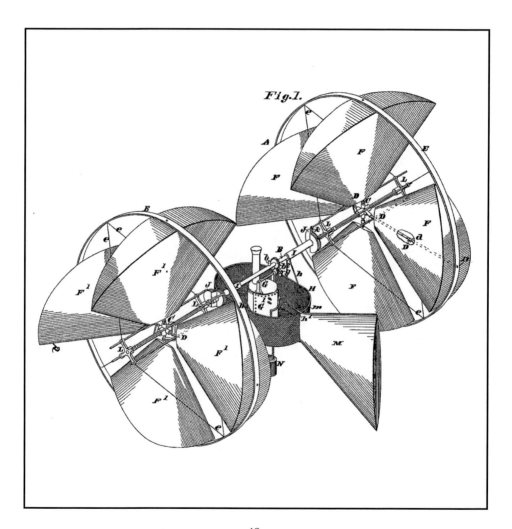

Fig.1.

Robert L. Downton
U. S. Patent 264,261
St. Louis, MO
September 12, 1882

Downton's invention was innovative, to say the least. A prominent feature of the ship was to employ a series of gas-chambers attached to a main shaft that could be rotated. The shape of the chambers, along with their rotation, was supposed to both help propel the craft through the air and allow the pilot some control in the direction it was heading. The power to rotate the chambers was provided by an engine that stood in the car (represented by the letter G in the drawing). In the patent drawing a steam engine was used as an example. The engine's water-tank can be seen suspended underneath the car (letter N).

Downton described the action of the gas chambers in motion as "being analogous to the movement of the wings of a bird." A gas-filled balloon, shaped like a rudder, was attached to the rear of the car to provide help in guiding the machine.

The main shaft, hubs and spokes that attached the chambers to the airship were hollow, allowing gas to pass through them to the gas-bags. This enabled the chambers to be rendered more or less buoyant as needed.

Downton's patent included another drawing, showing a car with only one series of gas chambers being used, the basket being directly beneath and the suspending rods extending upward to the end of the main shaft. Instead of an engine, a crank-shaft attached to a series of belts and pulleys could be hand-turned by the pilot.

It turned out that Downton's revolutionary idea was never constructed.

(No Model.)

C. E. & C. MYERS.
GUIDING APPARATUS FOR BALLOONS.

No. 318,575.   Patented May 26, 1885.

Fig.1.

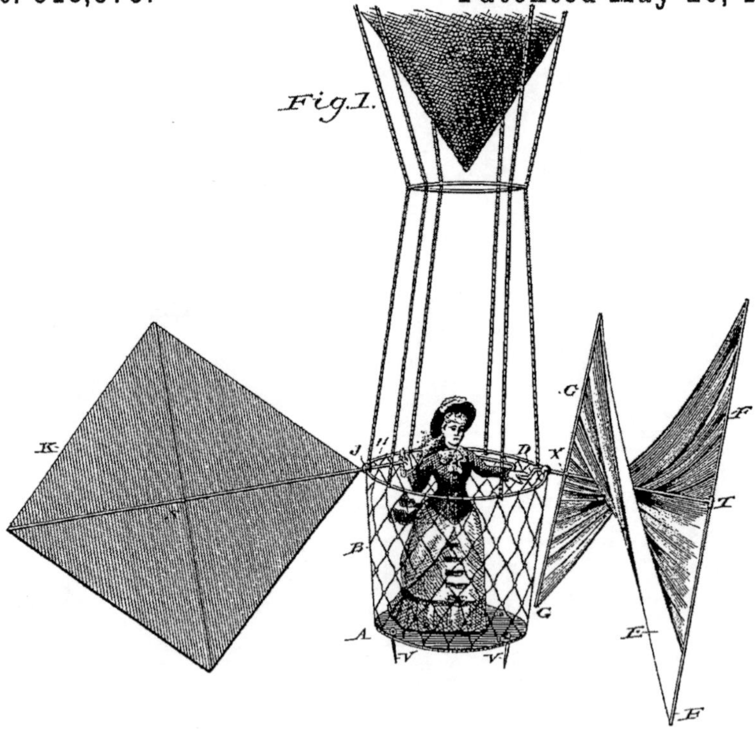

Carl E. & Carlotta Myers
U. S. Patent 318,575
Mohawk, NY
May 26, 1885

Carl E. Myers married Mary Breed Hawley in 1871, an intelligent woman who shared her husband's passion for aeronautics. Mary, under the banner "Carlotta, the Lady Aeronaut", made her first flight in an aerial balloon on July 4, 1880 at Little Falls, New York. The novelty of a female balloonist drew thousands of spectators to watch her performances. Mary made more ascensions in hydrogen balloons than any other aeronaut during her time. Five years later Carl and Mary "Carlotta" Myers were granted a patent for their idea on how to guide balloons. The patent drawing included Mary showing the apparatus. Mary was the first woman to have a patent on an aerial device in America.

The couple soon became financially well off enough to buy a mansion in Mohawk, New York. The "Balloon Farm" was equipped with a laboratory, machine shops, a loft for cutting out and storing balloons, and gas generating equipment. Mary retired from public performances in 1891. Carl continued working, and would later develop weather balloons for the government, as well as military balloons for use in the Spanish-American War.

Their daughter, Aerial, became a balloonist, as well. She would pedal a "Sky-Cycle"; sort of a bicycle attached to a dirigible that her father had invented, inside huge tents and auditoriums across the country.

The Balloon Mansion still stands as a monument to the couple.

Ringert Jongewaard
U. S. Patent 338,173
Harrison, Dakota Territory
March 16, 1886

Jongewaard's device was designed to rise from the ground and fly through the air using a propeller driven by the strength of the pilot. The pilot's seat was attached to a stiff triangular frame, which was mounted on three wheels. The rider's feet would push up and down a set of pedals (represented in the drawing by the letters *H*). This, through a series of a crank-wheel, a band-wheel, guide pulleys and other devices, would turn a set of wings above. An elliptical sail, made up of cloth supported by cross slats and a hoop, both helped raise the machine from the ground and keep it up in the air. Two rudders, one placed in front, the other in the rear, assisted in guiding the direction of the craft.

Jongewaard included an instruction manual on his ship in his patent.

"In operation, a smooth piece of ground being selected, the machine should be faced to the wind, if there be any, and the rider should incline the sail upward and begin revolving the propeller. Its action against the air will first propel the machine on its wheels on the ground, and as soon as the velocity causes sufficient pressure against the under side of the sail to overcome gravity the machine will quickly rise in the air. Now it is a matter of practice to learn just how to cant the sail and to turn the rudders under varying circumstances or guide the machine in any desired direction to fly high or low or to land at pleasure."

Jongewaard claimed his invention was "readily adaptable to the tall, the short, the weak or strong", a claim never tested since it was never built.

C. R. E. WULFF.

MEANS AND APPARATUS FOR PROPELLING AND GUIDING BALLOONS.

No. 363,037   Patented May 17, 1887.

FIG. 1.

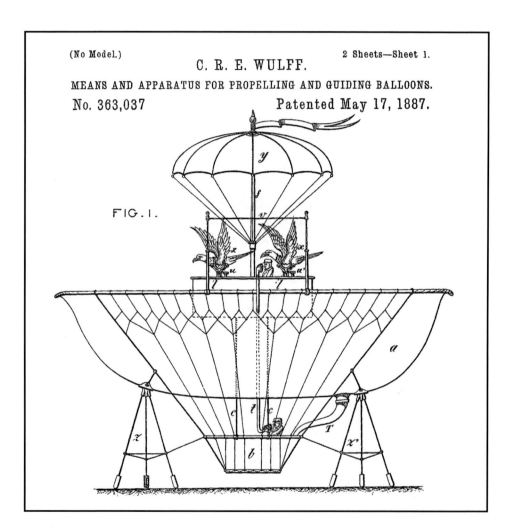

Charles Richard Edouard Wulff
U. S. Patent 363,037
Paris, France
May 17, 1887

Wulff's patent did not focus so much on how a balloon should be built, as on how to steer it once it was airborne. "All attempts heretofore made to guide or steer balloons have comprised mechanical, electric, or other motors for imparting the necessary speed and direction to the propelling parts." stated Wulff. "Attempts in this direction have generally been unsuccessful by reason of the weight of the motor and its accessories..."

Instead, Wulff had the idea of replacing the mechanical motor with a living one, that of a bird. And not just any bird, but those he considered from the "flying class", his examples being eagles, vultures and condors. Corsets would be carefully placed around these "living propellers", securing them to the airship, but allowing their wings to move freely.

The balloon (identified by the letter *a* on the patent drawing), would be filled with enough gas to lift the vessel into the sky. Underneath, a car for passengers, as well as the pilot, would be suspended. Above the balloon sat a floor, which carried the person who worked the device that controlled the direction the birds flew. Rolling rails, in the form of a cross, connected to the bird's corsets at one end, the other to a crank centered in the middle of the floor. At the direction of the pilot underneath, the man above could turn the crank to position the birds in the direction the aircraft needed to be propelled. Wulff recommended that no less than four birds be used, with one attached to each of the four corners of the cross.

Wulff's bird-brained idea never soared where eagles dare to fly.

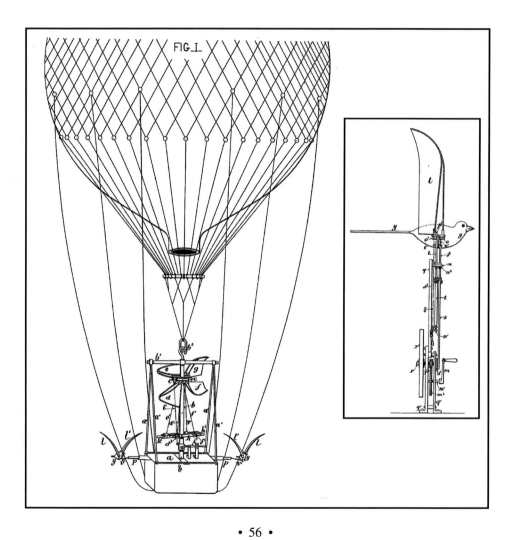

Blaise Bontems

U. S. Patent 381,106
Paris, France
April 17, 1888

Less than a year later, another inventor from Paris, France was granted a United States patent for a "new and useful Improved Apparatus for Aerial Navigation." Evidently, Bontems' idea was considered so revolutionary that he had already been granted patents on it in five other countries - France, Belgium, England, Italy and Germany.

"Nature in the form of a bird presenting the best model to follow in the construction of machines for aerial navigation, I have closely followed the movements of the bird in its flight as being the best means of solving the difficult problem of how to direct a machine through the air in any desired direction." stated Bontems in his patent. This solution called for the use of two arbors attached to a post. To each arbor was secured two wings. Each wing had a crank to turn it. Through a series of rods and gears, the wings could be moved individually or as a group. When the wings moved, they forced the air rearward.

Two bird-shaped devices (see insert) were connected by a shaft to a cranking device which, when turned, led to the "symmetrical beating of the wings." Each bird's tail acted like a rudder, which was controlled by the action of a cord connected to another crank. With the use of the wings on the central shaft, and the bird-like devices attached to the sides of the car, Bontems claimed that the ship could hover in the air, rise, descend or move to the right or left. In case it didn't work, (and it didn't), he also claimed it could be applied to toys.

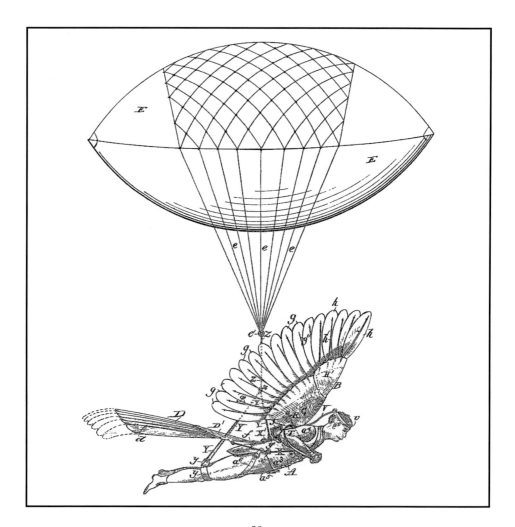

Reuben Jasper Spalding
U. S. Patent 398,984
Rosita, CO
March 5, 1889

Although the drawing to the left may appear to be merely a man with wings strapped to a balloon, it isn't as simple as it seems. In fact, Spalding needed twelve pages of drawings and text to describe his patented "flying-machine". Nearly every strap, belt, rivet, tab, spring, plate, fulcrum-pin, button, pulley, eye-loop, feather, pull-rod, cross-bar, handle and elastic band is described in detail. He also made sure to keep his options as open as possible. One example describes how the wing and tail feathers should be made:

"For instance, I may use silk stretched over a light frame and held to the stems or rods of the feathers... or I may use rawhide cut into proper form and fastened to and between light flat metal or wood plates, which are riveted to the frame... or I may use thin plates of metal of proper shape and riveted to short plates, which will be held to the frame of the wing..."

The balloon was an option as well. Spalding stated that he could see the wings being used by an "aeronaut" to propel himself through the air while "suspended from a pulley running on a wire stretched across a chasm", or applied "to vehicles or ice or water boats or an air-boat or frame-work, and the wings may be operated by man or animal or electro-magnetic or..."

You get the idea.

The wings were supposed to work like those of an eagle, the tail as a rudder. However, no description is given on how the pilot was supposed to get down after being hoisted in the air by a balloon full of gas.

Some say he's up there still...

Nicholas H. Borgfeldt
U. S. Patent 411,779
Brooklyn, NY
October 1, 1889

Borgfeldt's invention differed from the balloons that had been patented before it. Not only did he claim that it would "move up into and along in the atmospheric strata", the aircraft could also be used on water if necessary.

The car carried both passengers and crew, and was suspended by ropes to a cigar-shaped balloon. The balloon was to be filled with just enough gas to help support the weight of the aircraft; the series of wings jutting out from the sides of the car to be used for elevation. The wings were attached to rods that ran to the center of the car. These rods were themselves connected to a long bar that ran the length of the vessel. People standing on the floor of the car were supposed to grasp the rods that ran from the wings and move them up and down, sort of the reverse of rowing a ship. The middle lever helped keep the wings in line so that they moved as a group as they flapped. Borgfeldt's patent drawing included six men in sailor suits to represent how the crew were to be positioned on the "deck", but he also stated that machinery could be substituted for the raising and lowering of the wings instead.

The car itself was to be fashioned to resemble "the skeleton of a ship with raised bow and stern and with a bottom platform... on which the men or machinery for operating the wings can stand." Long, hollow cylinders filled with air were attached to the bottom of the platform, which would act like floats for preventing the car from sinking in case it should strike water.

Borgfeldt's idea was never constructed and sunk without a trace.

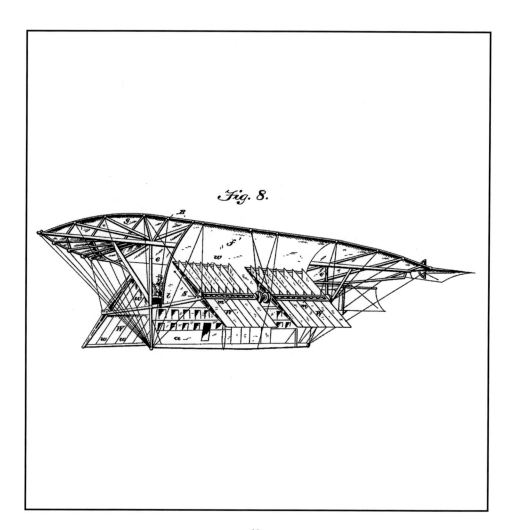

Fig. 8.

Matthias H. Baldwin
U. S. Patent 423,980
Memphis, TN
March 25, 1890

Baldwin's airship was over three stories high, the interior divided into three or more apartments with doors and windows. The central compartment contained the motor, the others were reserved for passengers and their baggage. Above the vessel was a large kite-shaped canopy, extending out over the sides and ends of the coach. The canopy helped to both steady the aircraft and act like a parachute if case of engine failure. A horizontal rudder at the rear of the canopy helped direct the course.

Along each side were parallel shafts to which were attached a series of wings (marked by the letter *W* in the drawing). A gasoline engine was recommended as the most probable means to power the revolution of the wings. Baldwin was in hopes that the rotary movement of the appendages would "produce a lifting and propelling effect similar to that produced by the stroke or movement of a bird's wing in flying."

The space between the deck of the coach and canopy above was to be equal in height to about half the height of the entire ship. The sides of this area were partly closed by the extending sides of the coach. The steering apparatus and lines connecting to the rear rudder was located on the deck of the coach. Two men were also to be stationed on this part of the deck, one acting as a pilot, the other as a lookout.

Baldwin's ship never had a chance of flying. It would be decades before anything as large as what he envisioned would take to the skies.

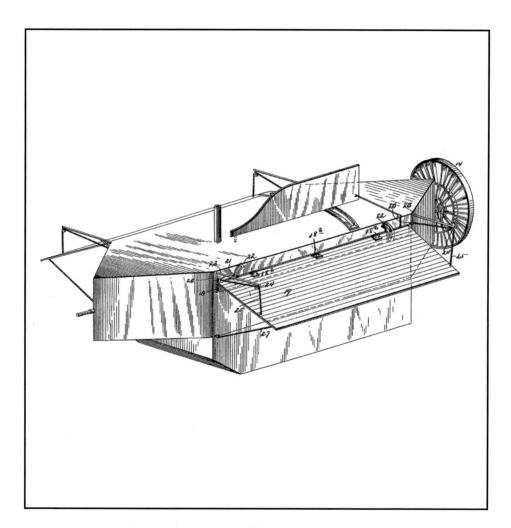

John Arbtin
U. S. Patent 462,612
Des Moines, IA
November 3, 1891

One of the objectives of Arbtin's invention was to simplify and improve the construction of future airships. The inventor suggested that the framework of the vessel be constructed of bars made of aluminum, iron or steel. The frame would then be covered with a material impervious to air and filled with gas to give it buoyancy. A chamber underneath would carry a steam-boiler and a steam-engine, which would run the propeller located to the rear of the ship.

Each side of the vehicle had a wing attached to it by a series of hinges. A number of arms also extended out from the top of the gas-receptacle area, which used ropes and pulleys to raise and lower the wings. As the machine rose, the pilot spread the wings out until they achieved the angle he wanted. The rear propeller was then set in motion by the steam-engine, which caused the ship to move forward in a straight line. A rudder, located on top of the aircraft, could be pivoted to control movement from right to left.

Ascent or descent was made by changing the right angles of the wings, which could also be pivoted end to end. To ascend, the front end of the wings would be elevated and the rear end lowered, causing the air to be forced under the wings and the ship to rise. A reverse movement would cause the apparatus to descend.

It is just as well that Arbtin's device was never built. What with the weight of an iron or steel frame, iron steam-boiler, iron steam engine, and the fuel needed to fire the boiler, it gives new meaning to the term "lead" balloon.

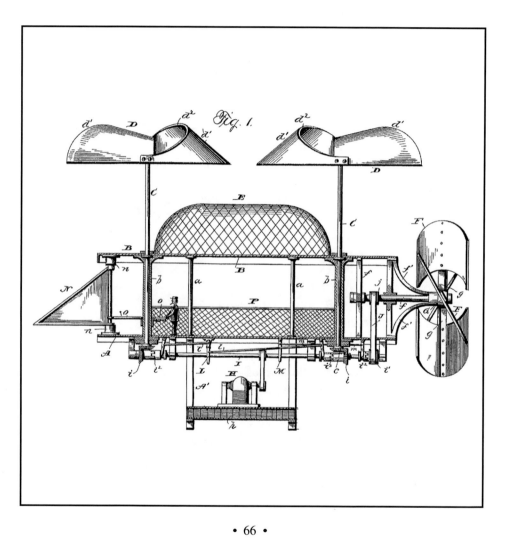

Fig. 1.

Emory B. Sowers
U. S. Patent 504,631
Westville, OH
September 5, 1893

Sowers knew that the weight of an aircraft could mean the difference between flight or failure. In his patent, he stressed that the vehicle should be of "a light and strong construction," although admittedly he never mentioned as to how this should be accomplished.

Attached to the top roof of the machine was an elongated bag, which was filled with gas. Nothing new there. But underneath, instead of a car, Sowers recommended a floor surrounded by a rail to hold passengers. Instead of ropes, posts were used to connect the upper roof and lower floor of the ship.

A hollow column stood at each end of the ship, whose upper end extended well above the roof, where it carried a wheel, and whose lower end extended a little below the floor, where it carried a beveled gear. Each wheel consisted of several sheet metal pieces. When rotated in one direction the air passing through the openings acted on the inner surface of the portions, creating a lifting effect. To cause the craft to ascend directly upward, the wheels were made to rotate in opposite directions, so that any horizontal tendency produced by one would be counteracted by the other.

The vessel was propelled horizontally by means of a screw-wheel mounted in the back. All three wheels were connected by means of shafts and gears to an electric motor that ran on a storage battery. A pivoted rudder in front of the machine controlled right and left maneuvers.

Sowers' tri-wheeled invention never made it to the building stage.

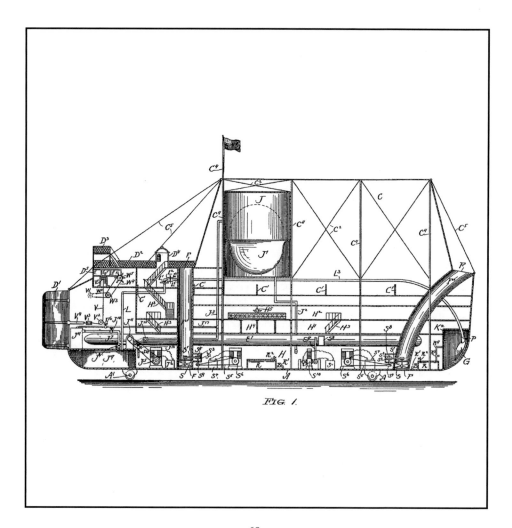

FIG. 1.

Edwin Pynchon
U. S. Patent 508,753
Chicago, IL
November 14, 1893

Pynchon's idea was that when passengers boarded one of his flying ships, it would have everything that could be found on an ocean liner, including a promenade deck, a captain's deck, passenger cabins with windows, and a walk on the lower deck which could be stood on to view the earth as it rushed by.

The body of Pynchon's machine was shaped after the pattern of a marine ship. The envelope of the gas-bag chamber extended slightly downward from the top of the aircraft, acting as a parachute during descent. A pair of horizontal "steering wings", as well as a large vertical wing that acted like a rudder, were positioned at the front of the vehicle. Vertical propellers recessed in openings in the body (marked by the letter E), also helped with the steering.

The most unusual thing about the design was the means of propulsion. After some degree of ascent and forward motion had been obtained, a pair of small cartridges containing gun powder would be detonated behind the vessel, the force pushing it forward. This would be followed by other cartridges of increasing size until the ship reached cruising speed. Concave detonating plates at the rear and base of the body helped diminish damage to the aeroplane from the explosions. Still, this would seem a bad idea for something that used flammable gas to fly.

In his drawing, Pynchon's ship is named the *Albatross*, after an oceanic bird with a large wingspread that is able to remain aloft for hours. The word also stands for "something burdensome that impedes action or progress", a meaning much more appropriate to describe Pynchon's unflyable invention.

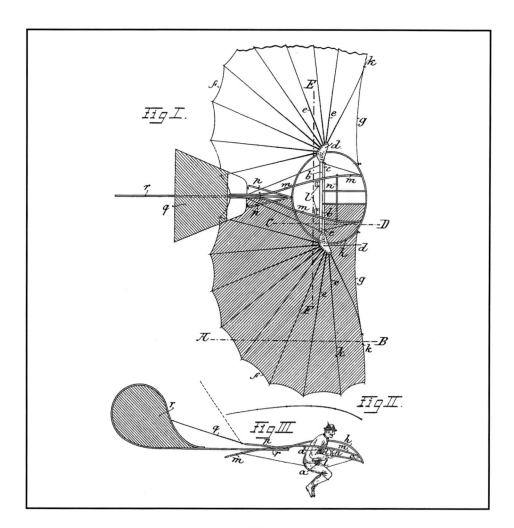

Otto Lilienthal
U. S. Patent 544,816
Berlin, Germany
August 20, 1895

Otto Lilienthal began experimenting with flight when he was thirteen years old, and continued for twenty-five years. His investigations were published in 1889 as a book called "Der Vogelflug als Grundlage der Fliegekunst" ("Bird Flight as the Basis of the Flying Art"). The majority of his experiments consisted of strapping himself into a glider and leaping from the top of a specially-built hill.

Lilienthal made over two thousand flights, some up to 1,150 feet, in the various gliders he built over the years. When he constructed his "Lilienthal Hang-Glider" in 1894, he considered it the safest and most successful of all his glider designs. In flight, the pilot hung between the wings by bars that passed beneath his arms.

Despite Lilienthal's faith in the safety of his invention, he met his death in 1896, following a crash in a hang-glider. A sudden gust of wind threw the glider backwards, depriving it of the supporting effect of the wind underneath its wings. The fall broke Lilienthal's back, and he died the next day. His last words were "Sacrifices must be made."

His efforts were not in vain, however, for two young men named Orville and Wilbur Wright read about Lilienthal's experiments and were inspired to tackle the problem of heavier-than-air flight themselves. In 1899, they wrote to the Smithsonian Institution for information about experiments that had been conducted up to that time. The rest is history.

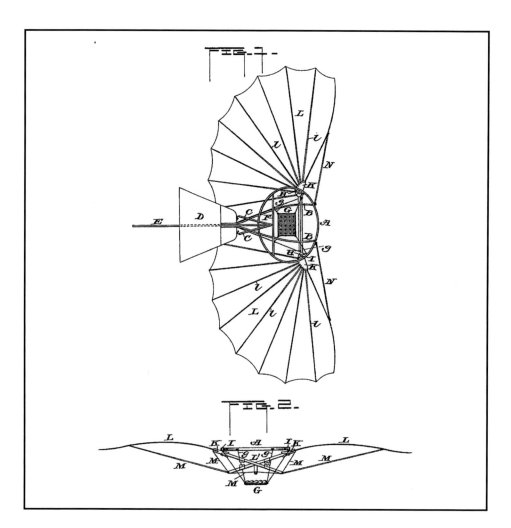

FIG. 1.

FIG. 2.

Octave A. Chanute
U. S. Patent 582,718
Chicago, IL
May 18, 1897

A self-taught engineer, Chanute was well known for his designs and construction of bridges and railroad terminals. While experimenting in material preservation he invented the method of pressure-treating wood with creosote, something that is still in use today.

In 1889 Chanute retired from the engineering field and began concentrating on solving the problem of flight. His findings were reported in a series of articles that appeared in *The Railroad and Engineering Journal* from 1891 through 1893, which were then compiled into a book titled *Progress in Flying Machines*, published in 1894. His use of the term "aviation" grew to become part of the English language.

In 1894 Chanute began experimenting with gliders. In his patent letter, Chanute states that his invention was "an improvement upon the flying machine recently patented to Otto Lilienthal..." The changes included a stationary seat for the pilot and a pivot for each wing, enabling the pilot better control and balance of the glider. Strong springs also exerted a constant forward pull on the wings, allowing for the wings to move forward or backward to compensate for changes in the center of gravity due to wind-pressure.

Chanute would go on to experiment with several other versions of gliders, some which were successful in flight, as well as sponsor the work of other aviation inventors. Such was his influence that when the Wright Brothers wrote the Smithsonian Institute for information on flight, the museum recommended *Progress in Flying Machines* as a must-read source.

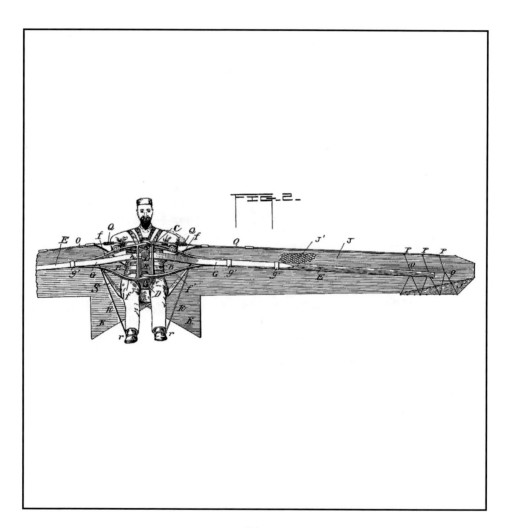

Louis Pierre Mouillard
U. S. Patent 582,757
Cario, Egypt
May 18, 1897

Mouillard spent a large part of his life in Algeria and Egypt. It was here, watching vultures soar in the sky, that he became inspired with the idea of flight. In 1881 he published *The Empire of the Air*, a book Wilbur Wright called "one of the most remarkable pieces of aeronautical literature that has ever been published." His book proposed fixed-wing gliders with cambered bird-like wings. He believed that there were two types of flyers, pilots who had the skill to maneuver an aircraft through the air and "chauffeurs" who focused on the engineering of an aircraft and who attempted to fly a powered machine before they had any true idea of flight control. His thought was that aviators had to first master gliding in order to gain the skills needed to pilot an aircraft.

Mouillard's 1897 design proposed to make the right and left rear corners of the wings double so that one or the other could be distorted to create a resistance to the air, enabling the flyer to turn the glider to the right or left. This would have been a vast improvement over the gliders invented before this, which depended solely on the twists and turns of the pilot's body to control direction.

When Octave Chanute learned that Mouillard was an invalid and without money, he furnished the inventor with enough funds to secure a United States patent on the glider, and gave him a considerable amount of money as well. The patent was granted just four months before Mouillard's death on September 20, 1897. Chanute, having been assigned one-half of the patent, chose not to build the glider.

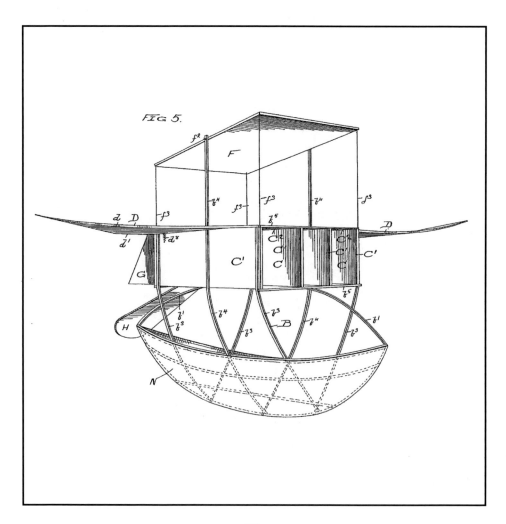

FIG 5.

William Paul Butusov
U. S. Patent 606,187
Chicago, IL
June 28, 1898

While Butusov's invention may look like a box on top of a balloon, it is in fact a glider. The upper part was a set of wings attached to "balancing tunnels". The lower part was a skeleton framework shaped like a boat, the middle in which stood the pilot. To the rear was a large rudder, mounted on the frame in a way that would allow it to move horizontally as required for steering.

With the financial backing of Octave Chanute, Butusov managed to actually build his ship in 1896. The glider had a wing area of 266 square feet and weighed 190 pounds. Dubbed the *Albatross Soaring Machine*, the craft was dragged to Dune Park, Indiana for its maiden voyage in September 1896.

While the glider was able to make it off the ground while unmanned, several mishaps prevented the machine from being tested with a pilot onboard. Part of the problem seemed to rest with the launching trestle Butusov was using. At least two attempts of flight failed when the *Albatross* was unable to slide down the trestle for take off.

The Chicago press was out in full-force for the attempted flight. This was partly due to the fact that three other men, Octave Chanute, William Avery and Augustus Herring, were also attempting to fly at the same time and location. But Butusov's glider, with its bird-shaped design, was the darling of the press. One newspaper reporter became so enthused that he reported the *Albatross* had actually flown with Butusov aboard, something that, in fact, never occurred.

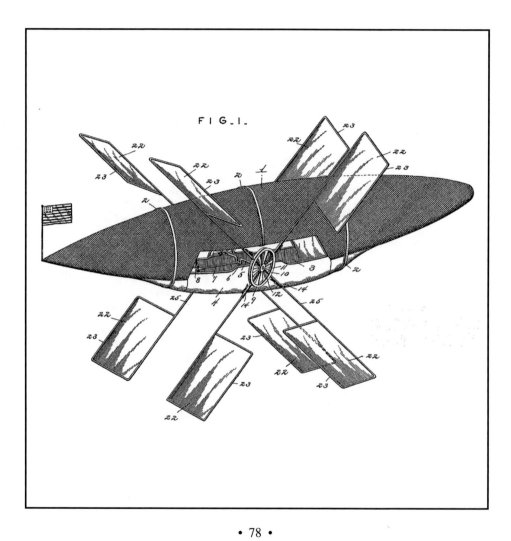

FIG.1.

Frederick R. Merritt
U. S. Patent 615,569
Prairie City, OR
December 6, 1898

Although Merritt's patent drawing showed a cigar shaped balloon, his invention was geared towards a guiding system that could be used not only by lighter-than-air vessels, but submarines as well.

The invention consisted of a drive shaft that extended across the body of the aircraft, with disks or wheels secured at both ends. On each wheel would be mounted "wings". These were constructed of metal; the rectangular ends being covered with fabric. The middle of the drive shaft was to be connected to an engine that could turn the wheels in either direction, this enabling it to travel forwards and backwards. The position and angle of the wings could be changed by means of a spring-actuated clutch-lever. A "shifting mechanism" would be used to extend the arms of the wings away from vehicle and into flying position.

Merritt tried to think of another use for his idea in case it failed as a guiding system. Towards the end of the patent he states: "While my invention has been described as a propelling and steering mechanism for airships and submarine vessels, it will be apparent that the same may be utilized as a windmill by mounting the frame which carries the mechanism... pivotally upon the upper end of an upright or standard and adjusting the blades so that they will receive the force of the wind upon one side or the other."

Quixote stood a better chance of succeeding.

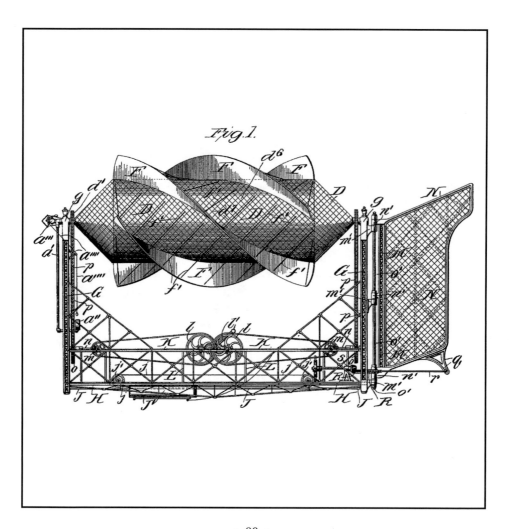

Fig. 1.

Joseph H. Dillon-Gregg
U. S. Patent 666,266
St. Louis, MO
January 22, 1901

Dillon-Gregg's invention was one of a kind. His ship consisted of a framework that was suspended from the axis of a gas reservoir. The reservoir was encased in a shell that rotated on roller bearings. The outer shell was cylindrical in shape and tapered at both ends. Curved, spirally arranged blades were also attached to the shell. A combination of drive pulleys, driving shafts and sprocket wheels enabled the shell to be rotated by a motor or hand-cranked.

Under the floor of the car was a series of guide-rods, on which was mounted a hollow box full of sand. This acted as ballast. In operation, enough gas was admitted into the reservoir to give the machine sufficient buoyancy to leave the ground. The box of sand would be slid toward the back end. As the airship began to rise, the front end would incline upward and be propelled forward. Once in the air and at the desired height, the weight would be centered and the ship positioned as horizontal as possible. The shell would begin to rotate and the blades would move the ship forward. A large rudder in the rear would control the direction the aircraft would sail.

In order to descent, the weighted box would be positioned towards the front end of the ship, forcing the nose downward. The forward movement of the blades would gradually propel the ship back to earth.

There is no record that Dillon-Gregg's idea was ever built.

E. M. FARR.

AERIAL VESSEL.

(Application filed Feb. 19, 1900.)

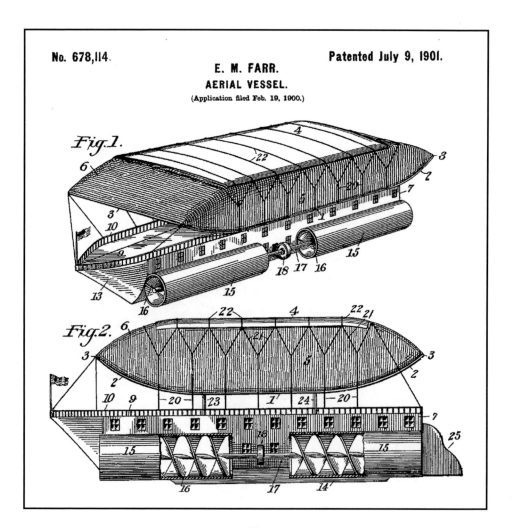

Eugene M. Farr
U. S. Patent 678,114
Washington, DC
July 9, 1901

Farr's idea was to build a combination balloon and airplane. Above and below the balloon were metal plates, preferably built of aluminum, for both lightness and strength. The greater portion of the bottom plate was flat, with ends that curved upward. The top plate was smaller, so that it could fit inside the bottom plate when the balloon was deflated. The balloon could be inflated or deflated while in flight by an "inflating pipe" connected to a gas generator.

The balloon would be fully inflated for take-off. When the desired elevation was reached, the pilot would turn on a set of screw propellers that would increase the forward speed of the aircraft. Once the necessary velocity was reached, the balloon would be either partially or completely deflated, with ropes holding the top plate against the bottom plate. In theory the bottom plate would then act like a wing, the resistance of the air against the forward inclined portion of the plate acting to prevent the machine from descending. Descent could be accomplished by either decreasing the speed of the propellers or by partially inflating the machine and stopping the propellers. A rear rudder helped control the direction the craft traveled.

One can't help but wonder what would have happened if Farr's invention had made it past the drawing stage. Would the ship have been able to remain in flight using just the bottom plate as a wing, or would air-resistance against the partly collapsed balloon have caused it to tumble to earth?

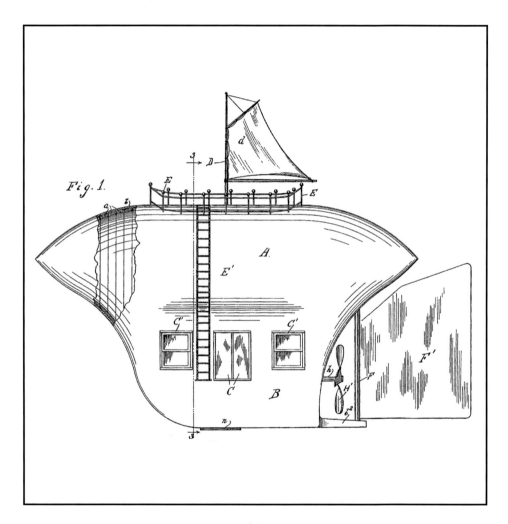

Peter Samorski
U. S. Patent 701,510
Chicago, IL
June 3, 1902

While Samorski's ship was meant to fly in the air, it was also given the means to swim on the sea. The balloon portion of his invention was cigar-shaped in form, with pointed ends. The balloon was constructed of a series of bands or rings abutting against each other at their edges. These bands were then lined on their interior surfaces with rubber sheeting to prevent the gas from escaping.

Thin and narrow strips of wood were attached to the outer bands, which came down and formed the cabin below. Samorski suggested that the cabin be provided with windows and doors, both for ventilation and light, and to provide an entrance and exit for the pilot and passengers.

Above the balloon was a mast with a guardrail. In the middle of the mast was a sail, which could be used for sailing the vessel while in the air or on the water. A ladder attached to the outer hull of the ship provided a way to reach the sail.

There wasn't much room in the cabin itself, as it was filled with a gasoline engine that ran, by means of a series of gears and crankshafts, both a rear and bottom propeller. When in water, the bottom propeller could be drawn into the craft and the drum containing it sealed off. The rear propeller was used for forward motion. A large rear rudder helped control the direction the craft traveled.

Samorski's craft neither flew nor floated, but it could have easily inspired the drawing of the Beatles' *Yellow Submarine*.

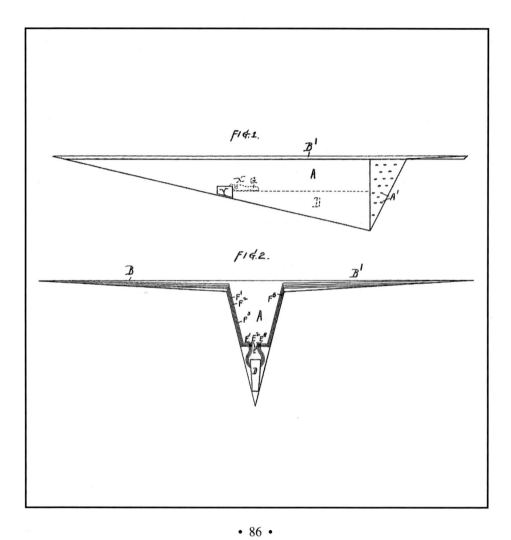

FIG.1.

FIG.2.

Theodore Gibson
U. S. Patent 710,266
Clarksville, TN
September 30, 1902

The shape of Gibson's ship would be familiar to any kid who has ever made an airplane out of a piece of paper and flew it across the sky. It was designed to fly almost exactly the same way as well.

The frame of Gibson's airplane consisted of a hollow, pyramid-shaped body, with hollow wings projecting from its sides. The pilot would lie face downward in a "casing" about a third of the way back (the casing is indicated by the letter *G* in the drawing). The casing was in two parts; one piece permanently secured to the ship received the lower part of the body, the other piece adapted to fit over the head and shoulders.

Gibson's aeroplane was powered by discharging expanding fluids through openings in the wings and body in the machine. A carry system of pipes supplied the expansive fluid from a storage tank to different vents in the ship, allowing the pilot to not only propel the vessel, but to guide and steer it as well.

In starting, the machine would be mounted on a wheeled frame on level ground. Fluid would be discharged from the stern and from under the wings, which would start the plane forward and into flight. A complicated series of discharges from the wings and back of the aircraft allowed the pilot to both propel the ship upward and from side to side until he reached his destination.

Even though Gibson included a set of instructions on how to fly his invention in the patent, he gave no indication on how the pilot was supposed to land. It never became a serious problem, however, since the airplane wasn't ever constructed.

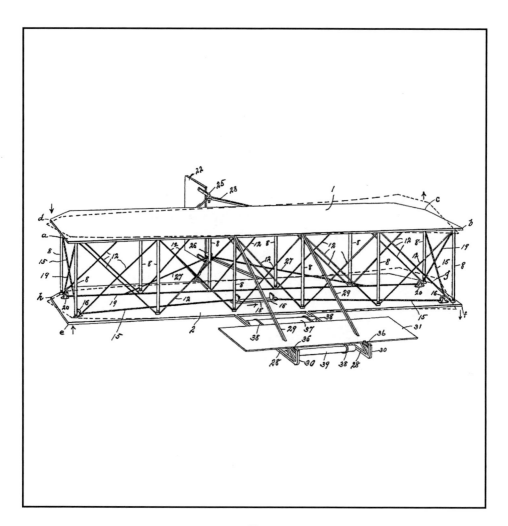

Orville & Wilbur Wright
U. S. Patent 821,393
Dayton, OH
May 22, 1906

During 1900 Orville and Wilbur began glider experiments on the sands of Kitty Hawk, North Carolina. It was there that they devised a method of warping the wings of their airplane to give it better balance. Kitty Hawk was chosen because of the strong winds that would help lift an airplane off of the ground and the privacy the area afforded them.

The next step was to find a power source to run the propellers. Needing to find a gasoline engine that weighed no more than 200 pounds, they turned to Charles E. Taylor for help. He worked on the problem for a month, but was finally able to produce a nine horsepower, four-cylinder engine in his machine shop.

The two brothers filed an application for their flying machine on March 23, 1903 without the help of a patent attorney. The Patent Office wrote back, stating that the drawing was inadequate, the claims vague and that their airplane would be inoperative. The Wright's response was to send a model illustrating their wing warping control system. Their patent was again rejected.

This didn't deter the brothers from trying out their "inoperative" idea. On December 17, 1903, with Orville at the controls, the biplane rose from the ground and traveled about 120 feet in 12 seconds. Man had finally flown in a controlled, self-powered airplane.

On May 22, 1906 the Wright Brothers finally received their much-deserved patent - with the help of an attorney, of course.

Aerial Inventions Patented in the U. S.
1844-1906

The list below includes over 200 patents for air balloons, flying machines, aerial navigation equipment, and other aerial inventions. The patents date from 1844 to 1906, the year the Wright Brothers received their first United States patent. These patent are online at www.uspto.gov/patft/index.html. In order to view the images you will have to download a special viewer, which can be found at www.alternatiff.com/. Enjoy!

Patent #	Inventor's Name	Residence	Patent #	Inventor's Name	Residence
3,799	Muzzi, Musio	Italy	132,022	Quinby, Watson F.	Wilmington, DE
7,207	Bell, Hugh	England	133,046	McDermott, Charles	Monticello, AK
11,248	Brewer, John W.	Cincinnati, OH	133,381	Moy, Thomas	England
23,163	Gage, James P.	New York, NY	141,785	Green, Thomas	New York, NY
32,378	Nelson, Mortimer	New York, NY	147,252	Francis, Otto	Grand Rapids, MI
33,165	Sherman, Josiah J.	Albany, NY	149,012	Wainwright, Charles B.	Philadelphia, PA
33,797	Quinby, Watson F.	Stanton, DE	151,124	Hartness, James	Detroit, MI
35,437	Crowell, Luther C.	West Dennis, MA	152,145	McGlasshan, Charles F.	Truckee, CA
37,667	Shaw, Thomas L.	Nebraska Territory	152,414	Rhone, Daniel L.	Wilkesbarre, PA
40,608	Connell, James H.	Lexington, KY	154,654	Dyer, Micajah	Blairsville, GA
43,449	Andrews, Solomon	Perth Amboy, NJ	155,218	Boswell, Lewis A.	Talladega, AL
45,665	Wright, A. G.	Santa Cruz, CA	156,359	LeBlanc, Felix	New York, NY
50,365	Just, Frank	Buffalo, NY	161,772	Fernandez, Peter B.	San Francisco, CA
54,992	Wooton, John	Boonton, NJ	165,881	Schroeder, Frederick W.	Baltimore, MD
57,996	Sykes, Chester W.	Suffield, CT	168,486	Hartness, James	Detroit, MI
67,739	Elston, J. A.	Elston Station, MO	168,788	Schmidt, Frederick W.	Hoboken, NJ
68,789	Quinby, Watson F.	Wilmington, DE	175,662	Carl, Daniel H.	Greenwich, OH
77,850	Stone, Zaphna	Kinsmans, OH	181,186	Lamboley, Francois X.	New York, NY
80,107	Abbruzo, Onofrio	Italy	185,465	Ward, John B.	San Francisco, CA
88,324	Morrow, William	San Francisco, CA	190,730	Barnett, Frank	Keokuk, IA
95,513	Quinby, Watson F.	Wilmington, DE	193,136	Beckley, Washington	Louisa, KY
97,100	Marriot, Frederick	San Francisco, CA	194,104	Murrell, Melville M.	Panther Springs, TN
99,629	Braun, Martin	Cape Vincent, NY	194,841	Pennington, James J.	Henryville, TN
100,415	Keith, A. P.	Easton, MA	195,860	Ward, John B.	San Francisco, CA
106,862	Oakes, Edward	Richmond, IN	199,334	von Ehren, Fritz A. L.	New Orleans, LA
129,401	Forbes, Isaac W.	La Porte, IN	201,200	Ritchel, Charles F.	Corry, PA
130,915	Haenlein, Paul	Germany	202,750	Pearson, William F.	Houma, LA

Patent #	Inventor's Name	Residence	Patent #	Inventor's Name	Residence
204,296	Cowan, Richard W.	Canada	320,042	Brearey, Frederick W.	England
205,319	Tracy, James	Waltham, MA	320,548	Foster, Joseph S.	Salem, MA
210,238	Cameron, John F.	New York, NY	328,218	Helmer, Nicholas	New York, NY
213,603	Apraxine, Count Antoine	Russia	334,866	Hunnicutt, Hurgar	Malvern, AK
214,546	Badgley, Henry	Fairfax C. H., VA	336,984	Beardsley, Levi A.	Dodge City, KS
218,573	Quinby, Watson F.	Wilmington, DE	338,173	Jongeward, Ringert	Dakota Territory
220,473	Greenough, John J.	Syracuse, NY	340,610	Patterson, William	San Francisco, CA
224,510	Blackman, Albert L.	Nashville, TN	350,303	Hamon, Augustin Henri	France
234,947	Brearey, Frederick W.	England	352,298	Cole, Moses S.	Nicaragua
235,040	Sullivan, Charles A.	Starkville, MS	353,193	Appling, Marby P.	Campbell, TX
235,792	Mackenzie, John F.	Scotland	354,413	Hartung, Otto Ulrich	Germany
236,619	Pearse, Edward A.	England	356,743	Braun, Martin	Cape Vincent, NY
245,768	Beeson, William	Montana Territory	361,442	Neubrand, Joseph	Long Island City, NY
246,872	de Jongh, Edward	Salem, OR	361,475	Wheeler, James M.	Fish's Eddy, NY
250,417	Blackman, Albert L.	Nashville, TN	361,855	Beeson, William	Montana Territory
252,955	Krueger, William G.	St. Louis, MO	362,605	Campbell, Peter Carmont	Brooklyn, NY
255,963	Fest, Charles P.	Philadelphia, PA	363,037	Wulff, Charles Richard	France
256,366	Peterson, Carl W.	San Francisco, CA	371,759	Hutchinson, William N.	England
259,464	Blackman, Albert L.	Nashville, TN	373,469	Morgan, Charles H.	Gunnison, CO
262,687	Myers, Charles F.	Washington, DC	376,937	Beeson, William	Montana Territory
263,397	Fest, Charles P.	Philadelphia, PA	378,364	Gustafson, Wald	England
264,261	Downton, Robert L.	St. Louis, MO	381,106	Bontems, Blaise	France
270,122	Ray, Joel	Philadelphia, PA	383,889	Johnston, Edward P.	Decatur, AL
270,939	Falconnet, Eugene F.	Nashville, TN	397,647	Holmes, John P.	Oak Valley, KS
276,012	Emsley, John William	Worchester, MA	398,984	Spalding, Reuben Jasper	Rosita, CO
280,914	de Souza, Jules C. R.	Brazil	399,271	Kunzel, Charles Aug	Philadelphia, PA
282,060	Debayeux, Auguste	France	399,783	Rieckert, Herman A. J.	New York, NY
282,647	Koch, Gustav	Germany	411,779	Borgfeldt, Nicholas H.	Brooklyn, NY
291,990	Davis, Kansas D.	Cole City, GA	417,755	Thayer, David	Boston, MA
295,157	Fest, Charles P.	Philadelphia, PA	423,980	Baldwin, Matthias H.	Memphis, TN
308,719	Wellner, George	Austria-Hungary	424,822	Pokorny, John J.	New York, NY
309,008	Thayer, Russell	Philadelphia, PA	430,343	Hennig, Carl G. E.	Paterson, NJ
311,885	Falconnet, Eugene F.	Nashville, TN	432,860	Cairncross, Stewart	Grafton, ND
311,886	Falconnet, Eugene F.	Nashville, TN	439,421	Nahl, Perham W.	San Francisco, CA
311,887	Falconnet, Eugene F.	Nashville, TN	460,194	Barnes, Burr Frank	Circleville, OH
311,888	Falconnet, Eugene F.	Nashville, TN	462,612	Arbtin, John	Des Moines, IA
312,344	Falconnet, Eugene F.	Nashville, TN	464,851	Cairncross, Stewart	Grafton, ND
318,575	Myers, Carl E.	Mohawk, NY	473,344	Riddle, William Nelson	Crowley, TX
319,758	Spier, Anton	St. Louis, MO	478,905	Barnes, Burr Frank	Circleville, OH
319,936	Stout, David	St. Louis, MO	500,326	Gabrielii, Georg Theodor	Norway

Patent #	Inventor's Name	Residence	Patent #	Inventor's Name	Residence
502,168	Battey, Sumter B.	New York, NY	668,375	Hubbard, Aristarchus F.	Simmler, CA
504,631	Sowers, Emory B.	Westville, OH	670,807	Olsen, Ole	Oakland, CA
505,414	Smith, Charles Abbott	San Francisco, CA	678,114	Farr, Eugene M.	Washington, DC
506,969	Bergqvist, Axel F.	Fairfield, IA	688,584	Botts, Robert Henry	New Mexico Territory
507,609	Billwiller, Carl Friedrich	Switzerland	693,943	Bell, Walter J.	Los Angeles, CA
508,753	Pynchon, Edwin	Chicago, IL	695,580	Richmond, Cassius M.	New York, NY
510,492	Smovski, Joachim A.	Russia	698,634	Conyne, Silas J.	Chicago, IL
514,287	Spaeth, Sigmund	Falls City, NE	701,359	Klotz, Carl F. A.	Indianapolis, IN
514,408	Blanchard, Jerome B.	Highlands, CO	701,510	Samorski, Peter	Chicago, IL
516,265	Cross, Christopher	Erie, IL	704,375	Rice, Joel Trout	Hot Springs, AK
526,394	Hurlbut, Duane	Paterson, NJ	706,832	Lancaster, Isreal	Chicago, IL
530,219	Borgfeldt, Nicholas H.	Brooklyn, NY	710,266	Gibon, Theodor	Clarksville, TN
536,174	Funcheon, Daniel C.	Valverde, CO	722,516	Johnston, Edward P.	Highlands, CO
542,100	De Los Olivos, Estan.	New York, NY	723,636	Berry, John	St. Louis, MO
544,816	Lilienthal, Otto	Germany	727,377	Kaehler, Otto A.	Detroit, MI
551,995	De Los Olivos, Estan.	New York, NY	729,800	Shultz, George D.	Kansas City, MO
552,443	Pennington, Edward J.	Mount Carmel, IL	730,107	Gibon, Theodor	Clarksville, TN
556,621	Coutinho, Manoel Vianna	Brazil	737,947	Morris, Isaac I.	Mellette, SD
573,549	St. Croix, Edward J.	Seattle, WA	741,568	Deventer, Charles Evan	Springfield, IL
581,218	Myers, Carl Edgar	Mohawk, NY	757,012	Bell, Alexander Graham	Washington, DC
582,718	Chanute, Octave	Chicago, IL	761,053	Morrison, Charles F.	Cornplanter, PA
582,757	Mouillard, Louis Pierre	Egypt	762,273	Best, Samuel T.	Louisville, KY
588,556	Crepar, Thomas M.	Grand Rapids, MI	764,198	McFarland, James D.	Fruitvale, CA
591,692	Reed, Daniel	Eagle Lake, MN	766,021	Craig, Stephen Merrill	Moscow, ID
592,704	Graybill, Jacob D.	New Orleans, LA	769,034	de Walden, Howard	England
596,231	Richardson, James	New York, NY	769,721	Thompson, George W.	Indian Territory
600,878	Leibbrand, Theodore	Columbus, OH	770,626	Bell, Alexander Graham	Washington, DC
605,579	Jone, Friedrich A.	Germany	784,161	Honeywell, Henry E.	St. Louis, MO
606,187	Butusov, William Paul	Chicago, IL	785,717	Criswell, Alexander P.	Chicago, IL
606,942	Rice, Joel Trout	Hot Springs, AK	785,740	Lancaster, Isreal	Chicago, IL
607,240	Hite, C. E.	Philadelphia, PA	786,932	Wood, Edwin F.	Colfax, IA
610,843	Brown, Thomas J.	Sedallia, MO	792,154	McMullen, George	Australia
612,808	Smith, Oscar L.	New York, NY	792,933	Schweers, Johann G.	New York, NY
615,569	Merritt, Frederick R.	Prairie City, OR	797,154	Spies, John	Philadelphia, PA
621,195	Zepplin, Graf Ferdinand	Germany	798,007	Branch, Willmer C.	Minneapolis, MN
641,793	Otis, Spencer	Omaha, NE	804,593	Friedel, Albert Hugo	New York, NY
648,634	Roze, Louis Etienne	France	809,093	Chiodera, Alfred	Switzerland
653,615	Cairncross, Stewart	Grafton, ND	817,442	Page, Charles F.	Pineville, LA
659,264	Stanley, Charles	San Francisco, CA	820,938	O'Kane, Bartholomew	Cincinnati, OH
666,266	Dillon-Gregg, Joseph H.	St. Louis, MO	821,393	Wright, Orville & Wilbur	Dayton, OH

-INDEX-